2, 4, LEGS

Patricia Brennan

Rigby®

A Harcourt Achieve Imprint

www.Rigby.com
1-800-531-5015

I see two legs.
They are walking.

I see four legs.
They are resting.

I see six legs.
They are moving.

I see eight legs.
They are working.

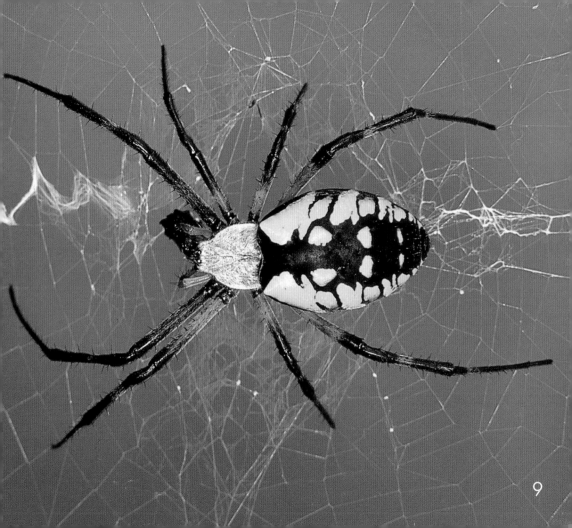

I see six legs.
They are jumping.

I see four legs.
They are running.

I see two legs.
They are skating.

Can you see legs?
I see no legs!